Toñis y Toño

Cathy Camarena, M.Ed., and Gloria B. Ruff, M.Ed.

Consulting Editors
Lourdes Flores-Hanson, M.S.E., and Gloria Rosso-White

Published by ABDO Publishing Company, 4940 Viking Drive, Edina, Minnesota 55435.

Copyright © 2006 by Abdo Consulting Group, Inc. International copyrights reserved in all countries. No part of this book may be reproduced in any form without written permission from the publisher. SandCastle™ is a trademark and logo of ABDO Publishing Company.

Printed in the United States.

Credits
Curriculum Coordinator: Nancy Tuminelly
Cover and Interior Design and Production: Mighty Media
Child Photography: Steven Wewerka, Wewerka Photography
Photo Credits: AbleStock, Brand X Pictures, Comstock, Photodisc

Library of Congress Cataloging-in-Publication Data

Camarena, Cathy, 1966-
  Toñis y Toño / Cathy Camarena, Gloria B. Ruff.
     p. cm. -- (Primeros sonidos)
  ISBN 1-59679-887-4 (hardcover)
  ISBN 1-59679-888-2 (paperback)
  1. Spanish language--Consonants--Juvenile literature. I. Ruff, Gloria B., 1971- II. Title. III. Series.
PC4159.C3776 2006
468.1'3--dc22

2005056908

SandCastle™ books are created by a professional team of educators, reading specialists, and content developers around five essential components that include phonemic awareness, phonics, vocabulary, text comprehension, and fluency. All books are written, reviewed, and leveled for guided and early intervention reading, and designed for use in shared, guided, and independent reading and writing activities to support a balanced approach to literacy instruction.

Let Us Know

After reading the book, SandCastle would like you to tell us your stories about reading. What is your favorite page? Was there something hard that you needed help with? Share the ups and downs of learning to read. We want to hear from you! To get posted on the ABDO Publishing Company Web site, send us e-mail at:

sandcastle@abdopub.com

SandCastle Level: Beginning

Ññ

ABCChDEFGH
IJKLLLMNÑOP
QRSTUVWXYZ

abcchdefgh
ijklllmnñop
qrstuvwxyz

Toño

piñata

muñeca

piña

bañera

Aquí hay una .

Aquí hay una .

Mira la .

Aquí hay una 🍍.

Mira la 🛁.

Toñis tiene una piña.

La piña sabe bien.

Toño tiene una piñata.

La piñata es un toro.

La piñata es grande.
La piña está encima de la piñata.

¿Cuáles de estas cosas contienen ñ?

Más palabras que contienen ñ

pañal

buñuelo

pañuelo

señal

leña

About SandCastle™

A professional team of educators, reading specialists, and content developers created the SandCastle™ series to support young readers as they develop reading skills and strategies and increase their general knowledge. The SandCastle™ series has four levels that correspond to early literacy development in young children. The levels are provided to help teachers and parents select the appropriate books for young readers.

Emerging Readers
(no flags)

Beginning Readers
(1 flag)

Transitional Readers
(2 flags)

Fluent Readers
(3 flags)

These levels are meant only as a guide. All levels are subject to change.

To see a complete list of SandCastle™ books and other nonfiction titles from ABDO Publishing Company, visit **www.abdopub.com** or contact us at:
4940 Viking Drive, Edina, Minnesota 55435 • 1-800-800-1312 • fax: 1-952-831-1632